PASTOR'S & ELDER'S HANDBOOK FOR

women's ministries

A complete guide for local church leaders

D1283473

Prepared and Published by
The Women's Ministries Department and Ministerial Association
The General Conference of Seventh-day Adventists

ISBN 1-57847-045-5

Contents

Forword

The New Testament clearly teaches the priesthood of all believers, with each member of God's family valued and called to share in the proclamation of the good news.

The qualities that united the efforts of the early Christians was their commitment to Christ's kingdom and their empowerment by the Holy Spirit to accomplish God's mission.

Women among Christ's followers included the Samaritan woman at Jacob's well who served as the first-recorded public evangelist; sanctified women who provided hospitality and sustenance to Jesus; and Mary who was the first to preach Jesus' resurrection—even to the other eleven unbelieving disciples.

Likewise, the early church grew stronger as women of faith united their individual ministries of teaching, leadership, prophecy, prayer, and proclamation to build and strengthen God's cause.

You will discover that this easy-to-read and easy-to-implement handbook provides a guide for pastors, elders, and other church leaders for establishing a spiritual and practical approach in the congregation to encourage women's ministries as part of the church's overall strategy to prepare people ready for Jesus' second advent.

The General Conference Ministerial Association is pleased to join our efforts with the General Conference Women's Ministries Department in encouraging all leaders everywhere to use every available resource and each willing believer for hastening the great day when Jesus returns.

James A. Cress, Director   **Heather-Dawn Small, Director**
Ministerial Association   *Women's Ministries Dept.*

General Conference of Seventh-day Adventists
12501 Old Columbia Pike
Silver Spring, Maryland, 20904, USA
www.ministerialassociation.com/resources
2007

Introduction

The book you hold in your hand is a condensation of the General Conference Women's Ministries Department Handbook. It was felt necessary to do this so that all our sisters at the church leadership level could have access to this information.

It has taken many hours of labor to put this together but we know that you will benefit greatly from the information we have placed inside. Please take the time to read it through and to know the history of this department, our goals and vision. But even more than that it will give you an understanding of this department and assist you to plan effectively for the women in your church.

We send this to you with many prayers and love, and know that God will bless your ministry as you continue to put Him first and depend on Him for wisdom and strength.

—General Conference Women's Ministries Director

CHAPTER ONE

Philosophy and Mission of Women's Ministries

Philosophy

The Department of Women's Ministries is committed to encouraging, challenging, equipping, and nurturing Seventh-day Adventist women as they do their part in carrying the Gospel message to the world.

"The Lord has a work for women as well as for men. They may take their places in His work at this crisis, and He will work through them. . . . They can do in families a work that men cannot do, a work that reaches the inner life. They can come close to the hearts of those whom men cannot reach. Their labor is needed."—*Welfare Ministry,* p. 145.

Vision

The spiritual vision of Women's Ministries is to know Jesus passionately and to serve and disciple other women.

Statement of Purpose

The primary purpose of the Department of Women's Ministries is to nurture, facilitate, and support women in their Christian lives as disciples of Jesus Christ and members of His

World Church. In consultation with administration and other departments of the church, the department shares the responsibility for developing a global evangelistic strategy and provides training to equip the women of the church to uplift Christ in the church and in the world.

"We may do a noble work for God if we will. Woman does not know her power. . . There is a higher purpose for woman, a grander destiny. She should develop and cultivate her powers, for God can employ them in the great work of saving souls from eternal ruin."—*Testimonies for the Church,* vol. 4, p. 642.

The Department of Women's Ministries will focus on the six challenge issues—identified by division Women's Ministries directors and voted by the Women's Ministries Advisory—as being barriers that prevent women from reaching their full potential:

- Illiteracy
- Poverty
- Threats to health
- Length of workday and poor working conditions
- Abuse
- The need for training and mentoring for greater involvement in the mission of the church

Mission Statement

General Conference Department of Women's Ministries

The Department of Women's Ministries exists to uphold, encourage, and challenge Adventist women in their pilgrimage as disciples of Jesus Christ and members of His World Church.

Our mission is in the larger sense common to all Christians—that of uplifting Christ in the church and in the world. But more specifically, we are called to:

- elevate women as persons of inestimable worth because they have been created and redeemed;

- enable women to deepen their faith and experience spiritual growth and renewal;
- build networks among women in the World Church to encourage bonds of friendship and mutual support and the creative exchange of ideas and information;
- mentor young Adventist women, encouraging their involvement, and creating paths for them as they reach for their potential in Christ;
- address the concerns of women in a global context;
- bring women's unique perspectives to the issues facing the World Church;
- seek expanding avenues of dynamic Christian service for women;
- challenge each Adventist woman with her potential to complement the gifts given to other women and men as they work side by side to further the global mission of the Seventh-day Adventist Church—that out of the fullness we as women have personally found in Jesus Christ, we may be empowered to share the good news within our families, among our fellow believers, and in ever expanding circles in the unsaved world.

Ellen White's Quotes About Women

"When a great and decisive work is to be done, God chooses men and women to do this work, and it will see the loss if the talents of both are not combined." —*Evangelism*, p. 469.

"We may do a noble work for God if we will. Woman does not know her power for God. . . . There is a higher purpose for woman, a grander destiny. She should develop and cultivate her powers, for God can employ them in the great work of saving souls from eternal ruin."

—*Testimonies for the Church*, vol. 4, p. 642; *Evangelism*, p. 465.

"There never was a time when more workers were needed than at the present. There are brethren and sisters throughout all our ranks who should discipline themselves to engage in this work; in all our churches something should be done to spread the truth. It is the duty of all to study the various points of our faith."

—*Review and Herald,* April 1, 1880.

"All who work for God should have the Martha and the Mary attributes blended—a willingness to minister and a sincere love of the truth. Self and selfishness must be put out of sight. God calls for earnest women workers, workers who are prudent, warmhearted, tender, and true to principle. He calls for persevering women who will take their minds from self . . . and will center them on Christ, speaking words of truth, praying with the persons to whom they can obtain access, laboring for the conversion of souls."

—*Testimony Treasures,* vol. 2, p. 405.

"Women can be instruments of righteousness, rendering holy service. It was Mary that first preached a risen Jesus . . . . If there were twenty women where now there is one, who would make this holy mission [one-to-one ministry] their cherished work, we should see many more converted to the truth. The refining, softening influence of Christian women is needed in the great work of preaching the truth."

—*Evangelism,* p. 471.

"The Lord has a work for women as well as men to do. They may accomplish a good work for God if they will first learn in the school of Christ the precious, all-important lesson of meekness. They must not only bear the name of Christ, but possess His Spirit. They must walk even as He walked, purifying their souls from everything that defiles. Then they will be able to benefit others by presenting the all-sufficiency of Jesus."

—*Testimony Treasures,* vol. 2, p. 404.

A Brief History of Women's Ministries

Work in the 1800s

While it is true that Women's Ministries did not become a full department of the General Conference until 1995, the Seventh-day Adventist Church has long recognized the importance of ministering to women, even as far back as the 1800s. Women's Ministries began in 1898 when Mrs. Sarepta Myrenda Irish Henry, in correspondence with Ellen G. White, outlined "women's ministries." She was granted a ministerial license from the General Conference and became the first Women's Ministries Director for the General Conference.

Work in the 1900s

In written form, Women's Ministries activities were not recorded from 1900–1970. This period has been called "the silent years." The first commission to study the role of women in the church was formed in September 1973 and met at Camp Mohaven in Ohio.

In 1990, 35 women, representing various groups, met in Pennsylvania to ask the church to appoint a full-time director of Women's Ministries at all levels. These directors would identify, assess, and develop strategies to meet women's needs; generate and disseminate accurate information concerning the role of women in the church; sponsor retreats for the purpose of spiritual nourishment; and direct activities to educate women regarding church governance and policies. At the GC level, this person would be a Field Secretary. At all levels, this position would be fully funded, with a travel budget and a budget to cover research, publications, translations, materials, and meetings.

Emergence of the Department

The General Conference session in Utrecht marked a watershed for Women's Ministries. In July 1995, the session

Mental encourage women
Paths for their involvement in
the church as they reach for their
Potential in Christ

Pancakes _ Making

4 Four
pinch salt

3½ sugar
1 table Salt
6 eggs yoak
2 cups milk   mixed e yoak
2 TS Vanella
3½ cup butter
eggs milk flour) together
mixed with wisp eggs white sepe
½ White ten yellow mixed
stressed with wisp then add
all white)

375° — greddle   1 stick butter to
wype, need spoon Fruits
Blue berry on topping
Banana Topping
walnuts Topping

voted full department status to Women's Ministries. Rose Otis was elected Women's Ministries Director of the General Conference.

Today, Women's Ministries has become a worldwide ministry with every division in the world field. Each division has a director who oversees the work of spiritual nurturing, mentoring and training for women.

Church Manual Statement

Women's Ministries exists to uphold, encourage, and challenge Seventh-day Adventist women in their daily walk as disciples of Jesus Christ and as members of His World Church. The mission of Women's Ministries is, in the larger sense, common to all Christians—to uplift Christ in the church and in the world. In doing this, the ministry seeks to:

1. Foster spiritual growth and renewal among women;
2. Affirm that women are of inestimable worth by virtue of their creation and redemption, and to equip them for service in the church;
3. Minister to the broad spectrum of women's needs across their lifespan, being sensitive to multi-cultural and multi-ethnic perspectives;
4. Liaise and cooperate with other specialized departments of the church to facilitate the ministry to women and of women;
5. Build goodwill among women in the World Church that encourages bonds of friendship, mutual support, and the creative exchange of ideas and information;
6. Mentor and encourage Seventh-day Adventist women, creating paths for their involvement in the church as they reach for their potential in Christ;
7. Find ways and means to challenge each Seventh-day Adventist woman to use her spiritual gifts to complement

the talents of others as they work side by side to further the global mission of the church.

Women's Ministries Leader—The Women's Ministries leader is elected by the church to develop specific ministries, to nurture women, and to equip them for service to God and to the church. She serves as Chair of the Women's Ministries Committee, encouraging ideas and plans that maximize women's contributions to the mission of the church. As Chair, she is responsible for organizing the agenda, moderating discussion, and developing group cohesion through personal sharing, prayer, and fellowship.

She also serves as a member of the Church Board, integrating activities and programs for women into the larger church program. It is her responsibility to keep the church informed of the contribution of Women's Ministries to church life. The leader's liaison for training and resource material is the local Conference/Mission Women's Ministries Director.

Qualifications of the Women's Ministries Leader—The Women's Ministries Leader should be a woman with a sensitive, caring nature, a burden for women's ministry and concerns, a balance in her perspectives so as to represent a broad spectrum of women, and an ability to encourage other women to cultivate their spiritual gifts. She should be able to work well with the women in the church, the pastor, and the church board.

The Women's Ministries Committee—The Women's Ministries Leader works with the pastor and church board to establish a Women's Ministries Committee to foster a ministry to women in the church. This committee should be comprised of persons interested in the broad spectrum of women's needs and services. To form a balanced team, the members should possess varied talents and experience. Major responsibilities of the Women's Ministries Committee will include the following:

1. To assess the needs of women in the local church and community, utilizing surveys and interviews and in counsel with the pastor and church leaders;

2. To brainstorm, develop strategies, and cooperate with other specialized departments of the church to foster programs and activities which minister to women;

3. To plan and implement these and other initiatives which relate to women's specific and varied needs, in cooperation with the pastor, departmental specialists, and other church leaders;

4. To facilitate local church participation in annual programs and activities initiated by the conference/union/division/General Conference, such as the International Women's Day of Prayer, Women's Ministries Day, and Small-Group Ministries to support and encourage them in service. Information regarding these programs is available through the conference/union and division Department of Women's Ministries.

The Women's Ministries leader is also added to the church board (*Church Manual,* p. 91), the Personal Ministries Council (*Church Manual,* p. 102), and the list of those who should be dealt with by the nominating committee (*Church Manual,* p. 142).

Women's Ministries Today

What it is...

- An opportunity for discipling, mentoring, and nurturing women;
- A place to address the spiritual, emotional, physical and social needs of women in the church;
- A place where women are encouraged to develop their

potential for participation in the mission of the church;

- A support system for hurting women—whether they are suffering from divorce, abuse, or loneliness;
- A forum to help address topics and issues as they affect women;
- A scholarship program to encourage young women to pursue their studies;
- A place where women are encouraged to become involved in all areas of ministry in their churches, their communities, and their homes;
- A place where young women are mentored so that they may find joy in the Lord;
- A place where women are enabled and empowered in Spiritual Leadership Training.

Women's Ministries wants inclusion of all programs

Women's Ministries recognizes that women have many gifts of the Spirit, and it attempts to help women discover and use these gifts to the glory of the Lord.

What it isn't...

Women's Ministries is not new. The first department of Women's Ministry in the Seventh-day Adventist Church began in 1898, under the direction of Mrs. Sarepta M. I. Henry, with the encouragement of Ellen White. Unfortunately, Mrs. Henry died not long afterwards, and the Women's Ministry department died with her. Nearly 100 years later, in 1990, the Adventist Church opened an Office of Women's Ministries which became a full-fledged church department in 1995.

- It is not a forum for women who have complaints against their employers, whether or not those complaints are justified.
- It is not a place to promote equal rights for women, although this issue is important.
- It is not a platform for the issue of women's ordination, al-

though we believe that everyone should use their talents to God's glory and should receive just recognition for work done in His honor.

- It is not about male-bashing. Women's Ministries strives for inclusion, not exclusion.

Six Challenge Issues Facing Women, with Ministry Ideas

The six challenge issues are:
- Illiteracy
- Poverty
- Threats to Health
- Woman's Workload
- Abuse
- Lack of Training, Mentoring and Leadership Opportunities

Illiteracy

One of the greatest needs of women around the world is the need to learn how to read and write. According to UNESCO, in the world today there are about 1 billion non-literate adults. This 1 billion is approximately 26 percent of the world's adult population. Women make up two-thirds of all non-literates. (UNESCO, 2001)

One out of every three women in the world cannot read and write. They are not able to read instructions, fill out employment forms, or read letters.

Additionally, illiterate women cannot read the Bible. This barrier cripples their spiritual growth and the spiritual training of their children.

When a woman learns to read, her whole family has a better chance of becoming literate. After she can read, she can be introduced to subjects such as Christian parenting and health. *"When you educate a man, you simply educate an individual; but if you educate a woman, you educate a family."*

Ministry Ideas: Basic literacy training, computer literacy classes, second-language training programs.

Poverty

More than 1 billion people in the world today—mostly women—live in abject poverty, particularly in the developing countries. In the past decade, the number of women living in poverty has increased. This problem is directly related to the absence of economic opportunities and autonomy, lack of access to economic resources, lack of access to education, and their minimal participation in the decision-making process. (Source: United Nations, FWCW *Platform for Action: Women and Poverty, 2005).*

Ministry Ideas: Small business development, money management seminars, preparing-for-retirement seminars, professional mentoring, time management, budgeting, support groups for widows, debt reduction education.

Threats to Health

Poor health undermines a woman's ability to be a fully productive participant in God's work. Globally, women's health is deteriorating.

Women's health includes a woman's emotional, social, and physical well-being. It is directly affected by social, political and economic factors. The quality of a woman's health directly impacts her life and well-being, her family and society. Yet many women around the world are still victims of poor health.

Ministry Ideas: Breathe-Free for Women, blood pressure/cholesterol programs, osteoporosis screening and prevention, exercise, weight control, vegetarian cooking and nutrition classes, cancer screening/awareness, reproductive health classes, grief and loss support groups, stress reduction.

Woman's Workload

Women around the world and in all cultures face the problem of work overload.

In almost every country, women work more hours than men. Studies show that in developing countries, women in remote areas can spend more than two hours per day carrying water for cooking, drinking, cleaning, and bathing; in some rural areas, they spend the equivalent of 200 days each year gathering firewood.

In the affluent world, women are expected to carry heavy workloads while maintaining family integrity. Balancing societal expectations for an intact and healthy family in a highly competitive work environment results in long days, limited rest and recreation, and little time for Bible study and personal devotions.

Ministry Ideas: Time management programs, organization seminars, management classes, small business classes, Bible study skills, seminars for working mothers.

Abuse

Violence is a global public health problem. Violence kills more than 1.6 million people every year. Public health experts say these statistics are just the tip of the iceberg; they maintain that most violent acts are committed behind closed doors and go largely unreported.

The World Health Organization reports that around the world, one in every three women suffers from some form of abuse. (Source: World Health Organization, Geneva, 2002)

Regardless of who the victim is, violence and abuse in the family is a serious problem that must be addressed by religious communities around the globe. No stratum of society is immune to the epidemic of violence. As a church, we believe that tolerance of abuse within the church is a denial of Christ.

Ministry Ideas: Abuse education seminars, women's shelters, support groups, healing seminars.

Lack of Training, Mentoring and Leadership Opportunities

Women's opportunities for leadership and advancement are limited in almost every country of the world.

Women have always worked, whether in the home, in support of their husbands, or for pay. They have always been involved in the church, although predominantly in supporting roles. Historically, women have held very few leadership positions in the Seventh-day Adventist Church. Currently, there is a growing need in the church for more women to be involved at the leadership level. This underscores the need to equip and prepare women for this role. Unfortunately, most women have not had the advantage of leadership training and experience.

In Women's Ministries, we seek to value each woman and recognize her individual needs and gifts. To be on the cutting edge, a leader must also be involved in continuing education and training. She must keep up-to-date on new leadership trends and look for new ways to minister to others. The Department of Women's Ministries has developed materials to train women in leadership.

The Leadership Program has four levels and includes 63 seminars with Power Point presentations, overheads, and handouts.

It is important that women, especially leaders, be involved in mentoring, serving not only as mentors but also as mentees. This ensures that each individual is not only receiving but also giving.

Ministry Ideas: Leadership training and mentoring programs, communication classes, seminars on parliamentary procedures, Women's Ministries committees, Spiritual Gifts seminars.

Women's Ministries Logo

The General Conference Department of Women's Ministries developed a logo not long after the department was born, depicting four women. These women represent not only the inclusiveness of Women's Ministries but also represent some of the objectives of Women's Ministries:

- They represent women of all ages.
- They represent women of different ethnic origins.
- ✗ They represent women working together.
- They represent women with a book. The book may be a Bible which is representing spiritual growth, it may be a literacy book, or it may be a book on any of the other areas of interest to women. The women may be learning for themselves or teaching others. They may be studying leadership or mentoring other women, but whatever the case, the women are growing and sharing.
- The women are supporting and caring for each other; together they represent an important part of the church, and together they can make a difference.

You may use this logo or you may adopt one of your own for your area, or the two may be used together. But worldwide, this is the general logo representing Women's Ministries. *You may obtain a copy of the logo on disk from your Division Women's Ministries Director.*

Women's Ministries Colors

Two colors have been chosen as the official colors for Women's Ministries; these may be used for the logo or any

other artwork, but you are certainly not limited to the use of these colors. The colors are:
- Aqua—PMS color #320
- Purple—PMS color #273

PMS colors are exact color tones used by printers and designers.

Ministry Resources

- *Revised Women's Ministries Handbook*
- *Logo Guidelines* (Booklet)
- *12 Things You'll Want to Know About Women's Ministries* (Booklet)
- *Women's Ministries: What It Is, What it Isn't*
- *Introduction to Women's Ministries* (Leadership Level One)
- *Philosophy of Women's Ministries: Roles and Objectives* (Leadership Level Two)
- *Women's Roles in E.G White Writings* (Leadership Level Three)
- *Six Critical Issues Women Face* (Six brochures and ministry ideas)
    - *Abuse*
    - *Lack of Training*
    - *Poverty*
    - *Illiteracy*
    - *Threats to Health*
    - *Workload*
- *Women's Ministries Mentoring Brochures*
    - *Mentoring Young Women*
    - *A Ministry for Every Woman*
    - *If They Can't Read, They Can't Read the Bible*
    - *Women's Ministries and Our Teens*
    - *Six Challenge Issues Facing Women*
    - *Finding and Using Spiritual Gifts*

(http://wm.gc.adventist.org or call (301) 680-6636)

CHAPTER TWO

Structure and Organization

Local Church Women's Ministries Leader

- The Women's Ministries leader is appointed by the local church nominating committee to develop and foster specific ministries, to nurture women, equip them for service, and build their Christian lives as disciples of Jesus Christ and members of His World Church.
- The Women's Ministries Leader is a member of the Church Board, coordinating WM activities with the church program.
- She serves as chair of the Women's Ministries Committee, encouraging women to share ideas, goals, and plans to advance the mission of the church.

Qualifications of the Women's Ministries Leader

The Women's Ministries Leader should be a woman who possesses a sensitive, caring nature; a burden for Women's Ministries and concerns; a balance in her perspectives so as to represent a broad spectrum of women; and an ability to encourage other women to cultivate their spiritual gifts. She should be able to work well with the women in the church, the pastor, and the church board.

Goals and Objectives

- The leader assists the church in meeting the spiritual, emotional, and intellectual needs of women in their various stages of life and cultural diversity.
- The leader creates an environment that encourages productivity, rewards effort and initiative, and provides a spiritual climate in which women can experience growth.
- The leader assesses the needs of women in the church through surveys and interviews. She chairs the Women's Ministries Committee, which develops programs and activities to meet the needs identified through these surveys.
- The leader is an active member of the local Church Board, disseminating information on women's activities and harmonizing these activities with the larger church program. She works closely with the pastor and the local conference Women's Ministries Director.
- The Church Board or Nominating Committee selects the Women's Ministries Leader in the local church. Qualifications include a sensitive, caring nature, a clear spiritual understanding of God's design for women, and a burden for women's broad needs and concerns. In addition it is recommended that the leader should have completed all or part of the Women's Ministries Leadership Certification Program.

Duties and Responsibilities

The major duties and responsibilities of the Women's Ministries Leader include the following:

1. Committee Establishment

The leader will work with the Church Board to establish a Women's Ministries Committee. The committee should be comprised of women interested in the broad spectrum of women's needs and concerns. The purpose of the committee is to brainstorm, develop strategies, and assist in planning programs and activities that relate to women's specific and varied needs.

2. Needs Assessment

The leader will work closely with her committee to survey the needs of the women in the local church and community. Survey questionnaires can be used to obtain this information. (See pages 31-32)

3. Program Development

The leader will work with her committee and the pastor to develop and implement Women's Ministries programs or seminars and to network with existing support groups active in the church.

4. Chair the Women's Ministry Committee

It is the responsibility of the local church Women's Ministries Leader to chair the Women's Ministries Committee. She will encourage ideas and plans that maximize women's contributions to the mission of the church. The chair will put together an agenda, moderate discussion, and facilitate group cohesion through personal sharing, prayer, and fellowship.

5. Advocate for Women's Concerns, Needs and Contributions

It is the leader's responsibility to keep the church membership informed of Women's Ministries and its contributions to church life. This responsibility includes allotting time during the Personal Ministries' announcement period or Sabbath School to share with the congregation at large. The Women's Ministries Leader is a liaison between the women of the church and the Church Board members, helping board members to view the needs of the women in the church, and to recognize Women's Ministries as a significant and vital part of church growth and church dynamics

Working with Other Departments

Women's Ministries should not work alone, not only because women are involved in many areas of church life, but because it needs the support of the other departments; it can and should also support them.

For instance, Family Ministries ministers to the family and the relationships found within families. We can invite Family Ministries to join us in programs that are of interest to both departments, and they may invite us to join them.

Women's Ministries may find many ways to cooperate with the Department of Education, especially on issues pertaining to young girls; or with Health and Temperance on issues of health that particularly affect women.

This opens up for women the possibility of working in a number of different areas/ministries/departments, depending on each woman's spiritual gifts. It would be helpful for the Women's Ministries Leader to build a good working relationship with the leaders of the other church departments and services, finding ways to cooperate and promote the overall mission of the church. All will benefit.

When working in such a setting, it is sometimes easy to step across boundaries or become involved in areas of ministry that are outside the concerns of Women's Ministries. Note that Dorcas/Community Services and Vacation Bible School are part of Personal Ministries and Sabbath School. It is likely that women will be very involved in these programs, but they still report to Sabbath School/Personal Ministries.

Ministry Resources

- *Effective Leadership in Meetings and Committees* – Rose Otis (Seminar)
- *Leadership Brochures - Set 1*
    - No Time for Another Meeting
    - What Your Church Says About Women
    - Organizing Your Women's Ministries Committee

(http://wm.gc.adventist.org or call (301) 680-6636)

CHAPTER THREE

How to Begin Women's Ministries in Your Local Church

Many women are interested in starting a Women's Ministries group but do not know where to begin. Other women feel unqualified; but in fact the Lord has wonderful experiences in store if only you lean on Him and become involved in a ministry which is best accomplished under His guidance.

Ask God to Guide You

The first step is to pray. Study God's Word and the Spirit of Prophecy for guidance; then talk to other Women's Ministries leaders. At first, perhaps only a few women may be interested in a Women's Ministries program, but as you allow the Lord to lead, others will want to become involved.

Work With Your Team

Gather a group of women to do preliminary planning. Be sure that the women on this committee represent a cross-section of women in your church—different age groups and ethnic groups of varying educational and economic levels. It would also be wise to include women who are single, divorced, disabled, etc., as much as possible. You will then be modeling an inclusive ministry and be better able to meet real needs. If the pastor's wife wants to be involved, that is wonderful. But if her schedule will not allow her to do so or her interests lie elsewhere, ask her if she is willing to serve as an advisor.

Target Your Ministries

Programs usually have one of three goals: to teach and disciple women, to nurture women, or to evangelize. Knowing which type of program you are planning to have will help you to plan successfully. From time to time, plan some Leadership Training opportunities for leaders and potential leaders.

Determine Priorities

You will doubtless want to survey the women in your church to discover what specific programs, classes, and outreaches your group wants; your survey will point out the real needs of your church. Check carefully that your programming will meet those needs. This is the formula for success that Jesus used in His ministry. He didn't minister just to keep busy, but He ministered to meet real needs.

One nice way to conduct a survey is to roll the surveys up and tie them with a nice ribbon, and then distribute them at the door of church. Collect them in the same basket after the church service. Do not let the women take them home; it is much too difficult to get them back! You may or may not want to have women sign their names. Once the survey is completed, select the most pressing need and develop a way to meet this need. Do one thing at a time, and do it well before you begin something else. It will help you to gain experience and to win their confidence.

Determine Resources

In planning a program, retreat, church service, or a simple tea, there are many resources to consider. It is a good idea to keep a file or notebook of possible resources: speakers and chairpersons; financial resources; and materials such as books, pamphlets, videos, or other educational materials. Your resources would also include information on facilities (especially necessary for retreats) and transportation.

Contact your Conference, Union, or Division Women's Ministries Director for a list of current Women's Ministries books, handbooks, newsletters, videos, seminars, or other resource material. There are many excellent books on topics such as women in the Bible, self-esteem, small-group prayer and Bible Study, women's devotional books, and many more.

Preparing a Survey

To help you determine the needs of your group, ask the women of the church to fill out a needs survey. Some of the questions that might be useful in the survey to define your proposal are as follows:

1. As a Christian woman, what is your greatest personal need or area in which you would like to see yourself grow?
2. What are the three most prevalent needs you can identify in your closest non-Christian friend?
3. Thinking about the women of your church, what concern do you have for them, and which group of women do you believe needs immediate attention? (i.e., mothers of preschoolers, single parents, working women, widows, etc.)
4. List three pressing needs or issues facing your community. How could the Women's Ministries of your church help to address these problems?

After you have defined the needs of your congregation, you can develop a specific plan of action. The Church Board should authorize a Planning Committee to confirm the ministry leader and team, or, depending on the time of year, these women might be selected by the Nominating Committee. This Planning Committee would then develop a proposal that includes a specific description of the program design, curriculum resources, budget, a starting date, and other decisions necessary to begin your program. It is all right to start small and grow slowly.

Women's Ministries Interest Survey

What subjects would you like to see Women's Ministries address? We need your help to know how to develop future programs to meet your needs. Please check all your interests and then prioritize the top four by putting numbers 1-4 alongside them, with 1 being your highest priority.

___ Aging

___ Bible Study Methods

___ Self-esteem

___ Small Group Bible Study

___ Single Christians

___ Child Abuse

___ Single Parenting

___ Depression and Suicide

___ Stress Management

___ Money Management

___ Teen Challenges

___ Grief Recovery

___ Time Management

___ Family History of Alcoholism, Abuse, or Other Trauma

___ How to Quit Addictive Habits

___ How to be a Christian on the Job

___ Women's Role in the Church

___ How to Live as a Divorcee

___ Women in Evangelism

___ How to Pray

___ Literacy

___ Eating Disorders

___ How to Mentor

___ Life-threatening Illness

___ Leadership Training

___ Public Speaking

___ Professional Image	___ How to Disciple
___ Weight Management	Someone
___ Women's Health	___ Witnessing to a Non-
___ How to Serve on a	Believing Spouse
Committee or Board	___ Prayer and Love Saves
___ Communication	___ Other

Women's Ministries Skills Survey

Please check all areas in which you would be comfortable sharing:

___ HIV/AIDS	___ Loneliness
___ Alcohol/Drugs	___ Public Speaking
___ Biblical Issues	___ Self-Esteem
___ Child Abuse	___ Sexual Abuse
___ Communication	___ Sexuality
___ Community Needs	___ Single Parenting
___ Crisis Counseling	___ Soul Winning
___ Death/Dying	___ Spirituality
___ Decision Making	___ Stewardship
___ Depression/Suicide	___ Stress
___ Diet/Exercise	___ Taking Care of Me
___ Divorce	___ Teaching a Skill
___ Eating Disorders	___ Volunteering
___ Emotional Abuse	___ Women's Roles
___ Finances	___ Working with Teens
___ Friendship/Dating	___ Health

Work With Your Pastor

It is wise to work closely with your pastor. During the early planning stages, talk to your pastor. You will need his or her support to be successful, and he/she can give you valuable advice. Explain that Women's Ministries will support the pastor and spouse in their goals for the church family. Never "surprise" the pastor; keep him/her informed of your plans. It is also important that you plan your programs into the larger church calendar well in advance.

Identify Spiritual Gifts

One of the goals of Women's Ministries is to help women identify and use their spiritual gifts. As soon as possible, help your leadership and the women to whom you minister to find their gifts. One effective way is to work in small groups. Have each group draw a picture of a woman (stick figures are fine!). Then have each woman write her name beside the part of the drawing with which she identifies her gift. If she likes to do things with her hands, she would write her name beside the hands. Perhaps she likes visitation—identify the feet. Perhaps she feels that she's been called to preach; write beside the mouth. Ears to listen, heart to sympathize, and so forth. Then ask each woman to share why she feels this is her gift, and if time allows how she has or would like to share this gift. *(For more information about Spiritual Gifts, see our Leadership Certification Program Level 3. There is a seminar available in this topic.)*

Write Effective Goals

Women can easily get carried away with an exciting idea such as starting Women's Ministries, but sometimes they fail to set realistic goals. Your program will have more support and will be more successful if you set goals. Ask yourselves these questions:

- Is this program Christ centered?
- How many people do we want to attend?
- What do we need to do to get this number?
- How many non-members do we want to attend?
- Whom are we targeting?
- What is our primary goal?

Put your goals on a written form. This will help you to see any missing links. To be successful, goals must be specific, attainable, and measurable. Ask yourself:

- Are our goals specific?
- Are they attainable?
- Are we looking at pie-in-the-sky, or are we certain that with God's blessing our goals are attainable?
- Are they realistically something that our women and resources can handle?
- Can we measure the success of our goals?

If you can answer each of these questions satisfactorily, you can be assured that you will build effective ministries in your local church.

It is always a good idea to evaluate your program after its completion. Did you achieve your goals? How can you improve your goals and your program next time? Go over each item in your strategic plan to see what went well and what should be improved.

Funding Your Program

This may seem like one of the hardest obstacles to overcome. You may be fortunate to be in a church where the board gives you a liberal budget, or you may have no money at all and have to be very creative. In either case, you will need a budget. If you are inexperienced, ask one of the church treasurers to mentor you in planning a budget. Get prior approval for all expenditures! Plan carefully and early to avoid surprise costs. Keep receipts of all purchases and maintain good records of all spending. Most important, stay within your budget or you may be required to personally pay for the additional expenses. If you're careful with your money and stay within budget, it will give your ministry a good reputation.

As time passes and the value of Women's Ministries is proven and appreciated, there should be money in every church budget for Women's Ministries. When your ministry is new in your church, you may not have the financial support that you would like. You may have to raise the money yourself. Women can cook. Women can bake. Women can organize musical programs. Women can have garage sales. There are many other ways that women can raise money.

The more carefully planned and successful your programs are, the more they can be seen as a benefit to the church, and the greater the chances that you will be to be able to get funding from the church for future programming.

Budgeting for Women's Ministries

At best, a budget is simply an estimate of the amount of money you think you will spend during a specific time period. Sometimes budgets must be revised during that time due to over-expenditures and/or unexpected needs that arise. The revision moves funds from one account to another while staying within the original budget.

Be reasonably generous with your budget, for committees usually reduce them, sometimes a little and sometimes a lot. It's better to ask for more and not receive quite what you wish than not to ask for it and receive much less.

In presenting your budget to the committee, do your homework and show the basis for the numbers and amounts you are requesting.

Keep in mind that all levels of Women's Ministries— General Conference, divisions, unions, conferences, and local churches—are responsible for using money wisely. Work closely with your administration.

Be sure to document in writing your Women's Ministries activities and their apparent results:

1. Women feel good if their church provides such opportunities.

2. Women invite friends who are lukewarm members to attend the meetings, and these friends experience and respond spiritually and socially to the church.

3. Christian women's retreats and meetings are significant factors in helping women to make a decision be baptized/rebaptized.

4. Women grow spiritually and become witnesses in their communities.

Always thank the Union or Conference administration in writing and verbally for their support, interest, and encouragement.

Sample Budget Form (for local churches)

Proposed _____ Budget for Women's Ministries
        (year)

EXPENSES   Date_____

  OFFICE EXPENSE

Duplicating	$_____
Postage	$_____
Stationery	$_____
Telephone	$_____
Other	$_____
Total Office Expense	$_____

MEETINGS
    Meeting(s) for Women $_____
    Speaker's Fee $_____
    Speaker's Transportation $_____
    Speaker's Lodging $_____
    Other $_____
    Conference or Union-wide Meetings $_____
    Total Meeting Expense $_____

PROGRAMS
    Advertising $_____
    Gifts/Handouts $_____
    Refreshments $_____
    Room Rental $_____
    Equipment Rental or Purchase $_____
    Other $_____
    Total Program Expenses $_____

TRAVEL
    Conference Spiritual Retreat $_____
    Total Travel Expense $_____

TOTAL BUDGET REQUEST $_____

INCOME
    Church Budget $_____
    Gifts/Donations $_____
    Fund-Raising $_____
    Total Income $_____

TOTAL NET INCOME $_____

[handwritten at top: Include Women from other churches]

Advertise Your Programs

[handwritten: on tv / Share information Church bulletin new letter / Posters TV announcement Radio New paper]

[handwritten left margin: ads]

Even the best program will fail if people don't know it exists. And people in the advertising field say that you have to talk about something *five to seven times* before people will be aware of or remember it. So think of every possible way to share information. You can use your church bulletin, newsletter, announcements, and bulletin boards. You can make posters and hand out fliers. If you want non-members to attend, you can use public service radio/TV announcements and newspaper stories or ads. Include women's groups from other denominations; every program should reach out to your community! Be ready for Christians and non-Christians, and be careful never to give offense.

You will be most effective if you can get your whole congregation involved in promoting your program. Ask the prayer bands to pray for your program. Most importantly, encourage your church members to bring their friends. Be creative!

Planning a Women's Ministries Retreat

Definition of a retreat: A drawing back, a regrouping, a "coming about."

Women's Ministries retreats are for women, organized and led by the Women's Ministries Director and a Retreat Committee. The committee is responsible for finding the following leaders as well as others who may be needed for a particular program: program coordinator, timekeeper, accommodation manager, meal planner, hostess for the guest speaker, equipment manager, music coordinator, registration manager, decorating chairperson, prayer group coordinator, and treasurer.

Purpose of a retreat

The purpose of a retreat is spiritual enrichment, fellowship, and an opportunity to challenge women to become involved with the mission of the church.

Types of retreats
- Local church, groups of churches, conference, or union
- Leadership
- Mother/Daughter
- Teenage

Venue for retreats
Youth camps, resort settings, conference campsites, hotels, recreational facilities, boarding schools during school holidays.

Who attends?
Women only, of all ages and from all walks of life. Speakers, musicians, session coordinators—all are women. Encourage the women to invite a friend or neighbor to attend also.

Theme
The committee may choose a theme for the retreat or ask the guest speaker to do so. Decorations and trimmings should be chosen to illustrate the theme. These need to be attractive and have particular appeal to women. A theme song, music, songs, introductions, and conclusions should all follow the theme.

Guest speakers
A guest speaker is especially invited to speak on topics of interest specifically to women. She is always given the retreat theme ahead of time and prepares her presentations accordingly. It is helpful if your guest speaker can arrive a day before the beginning of the retreat to meet with the leadership, so that everyone can go over the schedule and spend some time getting acquainted and praying for the success of the retreat. Whatever information is sent to your retreat attendees should also be sent to your guest speaker,

such as the type of clothes to bring, whether there is swimming or hiking, etc., so that she will be prepared to participate.

Time

Usually a weekend from Friday night to Sunday lunch or an equivalent period is convenient for the women who attend. Each session needs to begin and end on time. A timekeeper should be appointed to make sure this happens.

Food

If possible, food should be prepared and served by someone other than the women attending the retreat so that it is truly a retreat for those attending. A group could be hired to cater the event, or the husbands of some of the women may be willing to do this work. Sometimes one church can do this as a church project.

Costs

Obviously, a retreat costs money. A budget should be carefully planned and each woman charged a percentage of the total cost. If you are able to get money from your conference or union to help with the cost, be clear on how it will be spent and accounted for. Churches can set up sponsorship programs, or the money from the conference or union can be used to help those who would really like to attend but cannot afford it. Each committee should explore ways of keeping the costs down and of helping the needy. Costs should be kept as low as possible while still making the retreat an event that women will really enjoy.

Sample Program

The program committee will plan the details and print these in a program folder as appropriate, including titles of the guest speaker's presentations, special music/items, etc. When planning a schedule, allow some time for relaxation and time for the women to talk with each other and get acquainted without having to skip meetings.

Note: This is only a suggestion. The committee is invited to act creatively, and to implement their own ideas and innovations, to make the program fit the desires of their committees and the needs of their participants.

Sample schedule (adapt as needed)

Friday

4:30	pm	Registration
6:30	pm	Tea/Supper
7:00	pm	Music
7:30	pm	Guest Speaker
8:30	pm	Prayer groups

Sabbath

7:00	am	Early Morning Walk (optional)
8:00	am	Worship
8:30	am	Breakfast
9:30	am	Music
10:00	am	Guest Speaker
10:45	am	Break
11:00	am	Music
11:15	am	Guest Speaker
12:00	pm	Testimony and Praise
12:30	pm	Lunch
3:00	pm	Prayer Walk
4:30	pm	Workshops
6:00	pm	Tea/Supper
7:00	pm	Social Program

A prayer breakfast is a nice feature for Sunday morning; the guest speaker may be the special speaker for this, too. Following is a suggested schedule:

Sunday

8:00	am	Worship
8:30	am	Pack and clean rooms
9:00	am	Guest Speaker
10:45	am	Workshops
12:15	am	Closing

Prayer Groups

Participants can be grouped according to their birth dates, favorite colors, matched motifs, etc. The groups may be told when and where to meet for prayer, or they may decide for themselves, depending on the culture.

Idea: Heart-to-Heart. Provide hearts cut in two, following a unique design for each. At the retreat, the women are each given a half of a heart and must find the woman with the half that matches hers. That woman becomes her prayer partner.

Testimonies

This activity allows women to gain strength and spiritual encouragement from the testimonies of other women. Testimonies can include answers to prayer, inspiration from a book or magazine article, divine help in solving a problem, or praise and thanksgiving for blessings. Be reminded that testimony time does not lead to inappropriate disclosures or negative comments or criticisms of others.

Workshops

Workshops should offer practical help for issues faced by women in any aspect of life. These workshops should be presented in an interactive style rather than as a lecture. There should be one workshop planned for every 25 women in attendance, giving the women a choice of the workshop they will attend. Sunday's workshops can be a repeat of Sabbath afternoon's, giving the women an opportunity to attend any workshops they were unable to attend on Sabbath. There should probably be a minimum of four workshops from which to choose.

Alternative Saturday Night Activity

This could be an agape feast where a Communion is blended with a special candle-light dinner. The menu should be simple (fruit, breads, nuts, dried fruits), but the setting should be particularly appealing. Testimonies may follow, citing victories and offering praise and thanksgiving to God.

If you plan to have treats or keepsakes for the attendees, these should be planned and assigned. From year to year, different churches or individuals may take on the assignment of making some little item for each woman. These items may be placed on their beds before arrival, distributed at mealtimes, or shared during testimony or get-acquainted times.

Ministry Resources

- *Introduction to Women's Ministries* (Leadership Level One)
- *Organizing a Retreat/Congress* (Leadership Level one)
- *Advertising Women's Ministries* (Leadership Level One)
- *Writing Letters* (Leadership Level One)
- *Time Management* (Leadership Level Two)
- *Budget Finance* (Leadership Level Two)
- *Producing a Newsletter* (Leadership Level Two)
- *Writing Proposals* (Leadership Level Two)
- *Writing with a Purpose* (Leadership Level Three)
- *Women's Ministries Leadership Brochures:*
    - No Time for Another Meeting
    - What Your Church Says About Women

(http://wm.gc.adventist.org or call (301) 680-6636)

CHAPTER FOUR

Leadership

How to Recruit and Manage Volunteers

Working with volunteers is not a simple process. A successful leader follows certain procedures for recruiting volunteers, provides orientation to the volunteer's role, supplies a clearly written job description and training for specific tasks, and supervises the implementation of the task with generous amounts of encouragement for the volunteer.

Action Steps

Identify and Articulate a Need

The successful leader of volunteers must first identify a real need in her congregation or community. She then develops a mission statement that clearly states the need and the response.

Start the Recruitment Process with a Review of Current Helpers

How do they feel about their roles? Do they feel ownership of the program or event? Are some facing burn-out? Are they so excited about the ministry that their enthusiasm is contagious and pulling in their friends?

Evaluate the Pool of Potential Volunteers

How many members of your congregation are not involved with your ministry? Who are the professionals in the community who might donate limited services (such as a lecture or presentation)? Who else can you prayerfully challenge to serve?

Know What You Want the Volunteers to Do

Have a plan with clearly-defined goals, objectives, and role descriptions.

Schedule Training for Various Tasks

Don't be intimidated by the word "training." It doesn't need to be time-consuming or filled with charts. Your assistants need orientation about the role you are asking them to fill. A clear statement of goals and procedures prevents misunderstandings and frustrations later. When a leader delegates a task, she should also empower the other person.

Work as a Team

Learn What Motivates Your Assistants

Volunteers need to feel that they are making a difference. Listed below are the "Motivation Principles" for volunteers:

1. Make volunteers feel that they are *needed.*
2. Match the responsibility with the *interest, ability,* and *psychological need* of the volunteers.
3. Give the volunteers *meaningful* assignments.
4. Help the volunteers to be *successful.*
5. Make the volunteers feel *appreciated.*

Team-Building Training

As a leader, you should inspire the best efforts of your team in order to meet your organization's goals. Members need to know that they are valued, trusted, and respected. They need to feel like they belong to an organization. They need to know that the work they are doing is an integral part of the organization's functions. When all of this is achieved, we have cultivated a team.

Six Team-Building Activities

- Clarifying team members' roles
- Building trust
- Inducing members to contribute to overall department performance
- Sharing the recognition of goal achievement
- Enhancing members' problem-solving skills
- Using participative management techniques

Source: Taken from Patricia Murdock Miller's book *Powerful Leadership Skills for Women* (National Press Publication, 1988).

Characteristics of Highly-Cohesive Teams

- Team members understand and share the leader's vision.
- Group members respect and like one another.
- Communication is open.
- The group has a sense of team pride.
- There is little conflict in the team, and when conflict occurs, it is handled by using constructive problem-solving techniques.
- Group members are encouraged to cooperate with each other.
- Team recognition and credit for a good job is freely given.
- Team members understand and share goals, objectives, and mission.[1]
- Team building promotes a trusting atmosphere.

Help your Staff Grow

As a leader, you have an important message to give your followers: that everyone, regardless of experience or job title, should be constantly improving. Daily work becomes an ongoing classroom. Some ways to foster personal improvement:

- Attend seminars and workshops.
- Work directly with members to share insights.
- Devise group projects for cross-training.
- Visit other women's organizations or Women's Ministries departments.
- Develop or attend training courses within the church or conference.
- Encourage special projects that enhance skills and abilities.
- Read books, journals, and articles.
- Plan working retreats for your committee.
- Delegate work to able women.
- Conduct evaluations and get feedback; be open to changes and new ideas.
- Encourage questions.
- Praise, encourage, and nurture your members.
- Send members to Certification Programs.
- Help everyone to intentionally mentor as well as have a mentor.

Whatever avenue you use, the message you send when you encourage growth is encouraging people to expand their skills and knowledge.

Source: Heim, Pat, and Elwood N. Chapman. *Learning to Lead* (Crisp Publications, Inc., 1990).

Implementing a Mentoring Program

Jesus Christ chose 12 people from humble walks of life, and for three years He taught them everything He could. When He returned to heaven, He left the awesome challenge of sharing the plan of salvation in the hands of these disciples. Today, our challenge is similar, and Jesus is our role model for mentoring potential church leaders.

What is a Mentor?

Mentoring means that one person is having a significant beneficial effect on the life or style of another person, generally as a result of personal one-on-one contact. A mentor befriends, teaches, and inspires. Through her involvement with a younger woman, a mentor shares from the abundant wealth of her life: her knowledge about marriage, career, children, and interpersonal relationships. She encourages the younger woman to become involved and creates a path for her as she reaches for her potential in Christ. In a mentor, we look not for women who are faultless, but for women who have responded biblically to crises in their lives.

Setting up a Church Mentoring Program

Plan programs or meetings for groups or individuals on topics such as:
  a) How to care for children in church
  b) How to dress for success
  c) How to realize your Christian potential
  d) How to cope with life's stresses
Pair experienced women with women who need mentoring:
  a) Experienced mothers with new mothers
  b) Young career women with college women
  c) College women with academy/high school girls
  d) Grandmothers with young girls, especially those attending boarding school

Plan special projects such as secret sisters, friendship sisters, secret friends, and prayer partners.

Make sure there is equal opportunity and commitment. Make it an opportunity for spiritual support and prayer. Find ways to promote self-esteem without cost. Contact your Division Women's Ministries Director for more information about mentoring. A seminar on mentoring can be purchased from your GC Women's Ministries Department.

Source: Ardis Stenbakken, *A Model for Mentoring* (GC Women's Ministries).

Ministry Resources

- *Principles of Effective Leadership* (Leadership Level One)
- *Effective Leadership in Meetings* (Leadership Level two)
- *Mentoring Brochures – Set 2*
    - Mentoring Young Women
    - A Ministry for Every Woman
    - Women's Ministries and Our Teens
    - Finding and Using Spiritual Gifts
- *Friendship: God's Gift to Bless Our Lives* - Lou Blanshfield (Seminar)
- *My Spiritual Gifts* – Rose Otis (Seminar)
- *Spiritual Growth for Today's Women* - Rose Otis (Seminar)
- *Women Discovering Jesus* – Lea Hardy (Seminar)
- *Desire, Discover, Depend On, and Do the Word* – Dorothy Watts (Seminar Guide and Workbook)
- *Resources for Young Women* (Resource Binder – 2005)
- *Resources for Single Women* (Resource Binder – 2006)
- *Singles Seminar: One is a Whole Number* – Ardis Stenbakken
- *Woman of Worth* (Leadership Level One)
- *Teen Programs* (Leadership Level One)
- *Principles of Counseling* (Leadership Level Three)

- *Mentoring* (Leadership Level Three)
- *Personality Assessment* (Leadership Level Three)
- *Fellowship Activities* (Leadership Level Three)

(http://wm.gc.adventist.org or call (301) 680-6636)

---

[1] Manning, Marilyn, and Patricia Haddock. *Leadership Skills for Women* (Crisp Publication, Inc., 1989).

CHAPTER FIVE

Programs

As Christians seeking to follow the example of Jesus, we believe that it is important to do what we can to touch the lives of the people, meeting their needs, developing relationships, building trust, and helping them to reach their goals.

General Conference Women's Ministries Programs

GC Women's Ministries Devotional Book

The GC Department of Women's Ministries encourages women throughout the world to contribute to the WM devotional book. Submissions must be written from personal experience and share God's presence in the lives of women, or show how God works in women's lives. Profits from the sale of the devotional books go to the GC Women's Ministries Scholarship Fund to assist women in their educational pursuits.

General Guidelines

• Contributions on a wide variety of spiritual, uplifting, encouraging topics, primarily from positive, *personal* experiences of God's presence in the lives of women, will be considered. Sermons will not be accepted.

• This book is marketed outside the Seventh-day Adventist

Church as well as within the church; therefore, all terminology should be easily understandable and non-offensive to those of other religious persuasions.

• Authors are encouraged to submit multiple contributions; however, please do not submit a devotional a second time if it is currently under consideration for publication in one of the devotional books. If you have been notified that a devotional has not been accepted, please do not resubmit it unless you have made significant changes to it.

Note: *We cannot return unused manuscripts.*

• Those who contribute to this project agree that the profits from the royalties of this publication will go to the General Conference Women's Ministries Scholarship Fund. They further agree that they will receive no payment for any contributions submitted or accepted for publication.

• The publishing house retains the right to make the final selection of which devotionals will be published, and to edit all contributions.

Content and Format

Devotional submissions must be written in English; paragraphs indented; double-spaced; 375-425 words; typed. No poems, anonymous submissions, or pseudonyms will be accepted. Submissions are to be sent by e-mail if possible. They may also be sent on computer diskette or CD, saved in Microsoft Office Word, along with a hard copy. The author should include written permission if using material from other sources (e.g., quotes).

Biographical Sketch

Each author should include three to four lines of information on herself, such as occupation, church or civic involvement, other articles/books published, hobbies, and personal accomplishments.

Format Guidelines

Each submission should be formatted as follows:

(Upper right hand)
Name
Address
Phone Number

(Flush left)
Title of devotional
Bible text and Bible version used

How to Submit

By mail
> GC Women's Ministries Devotional Book
> General Conference of SDA
> 12501 Old Columbia Pike
> Silver Spring, MD 20904-6600

By e-mail
> womensministries@gc.adventist.org

By fax
> (301) 680-6600

In addition to being a contributor, you can support this ministry by buying the Women's Daily Devotional for yourself and for your friends, and by encouraging others to buy and read it. Make sure your church's Personal Ministries Leader is informed about the devotional book and that women in the congregation know how to get it. Many women have discovered a talent for writing and great personal satisfaction from having their devotionals appear in print.

Deadline: October 1 of each year for the book published two years later, but submissions are accepted at any time.

Please encourage women to contribute. We strive for global participation with a varied cultural and ethnic flavor.

General Conference Women's Ministries Scholarship Program

The General Conference Women's Ministries Scholarship Program was established to give scholarships to Adventist women who are committed to serving the mission of the Seventh-day Adventist Church, and who would otherwise be unable to afford a Christian education.

Who is Eligible?

Any woman who is attending or planning to attend a Seventh-day Adventist college or university in the Division in which she lives is eligible to receive scholarship funds. Primary consideration will be given to those in the last two years of college-level study. Scholarships are awarded on the basis of need, ability, and the recipient's determination to improve herself. She must be committed to serving the Lord in whatever way He directs, and dedicated to the mission of the Seventh-day Adventist Church.

Specific amounts of scholarship awards vary from year to year and are dependent on the funds available in each recipient's division. Scholarships may be obtained only through a woman's home division.

How can Women Apply?

First, you will need to obtain a scholarship application form and fill it out; include a photo, a transcript of your latest year in school, and submit three recommendations written by your pastor, church leader or teacher, and your current employer.

Mail all the information to your conference WM Director before the deadline date. If you have no conference WM Director, send the application to your union WM Director. If there is no conference or union WM Director, then send it directly to your division WM Director.

Applicants will be approved by each Division's Women's Ministries Committee and by the General Conference Women's Ministries Scholarship Committee.

How are These Scholarships Funded?

Prior to 2004, all scholarships were funded by profits from the Women's Ministries' daily devotional books for women. The first devotional book was printed in 1993 and was titled *Among Friends*. Since then, a book is published every year. By 2007, this project had raised nearly $500,000 to help fund scholarships for women in 95 countries. Many women from all over the world contributed devotional for these books. All profits have been added to the scholarship program.

Scholarshipping Our Sisters Fund (SOS)

In 2004, scholarship funds were awarded to only 50 percent of the applicants, and we realized that we needed to raise even more money for this program. A second program was developed to raise funds to help even more women. This new program was called "Scholarshipping Our Sisters" (SOS) and is managed by the GC Department of Women's Ministries.

Funds are solicited from businesses, retirees, women's organizations, and other interested groups and individuals. Donations may be named or unnamed. Donors may designate their donation for a particular field of study, country, or institution if they wish. Donations may also be given in memory of or in honor of someone special.

Contributions are distributed directly to the educational institutions involved. The money is divided equally among all the World Divisions of the Seventh-day Adventist Church that have a Women's Ministries Director and Scholarship Committee.

Leadership Certification Program

The Leadership Certification Program was developed to help the women of our church to develop skills that will enable them to serve in many leadership areas as we seek to fulfill the mission of the church.

E. G. White reminds us that *"There is a higher purpose for woman, a grander destiny. She should **develop and cultivate her powers**, for God can employ them in the great work of saving souls from eternal ruin"—Evangelism*, p. 465.

Developing and cultivating the abilities of women is one task of this department, and one to which we are committed. The program aims to equip women with the skills necessary to be successful leaders.

The curriculum is divided into eight subject areas: History and Philosophy, Biblical Studies, People Skills/Personal Growth, Speaking Skills, Leadership Skills, Writing Skills, Nurture Projects, and Outreach Projects.

Before certification can be awarded, the participant must complete the required courses in a particular level—these are called Core Requirements. In addition to these, the participant must also complete three other seminars of their choice from among the remaining courses, called Electives.

Following is an outline of the Leadership Certification course.

Level 1

Core Requirements
Introduction to Women's Ministries/Overview
Conditions of Women in Bible Times

Communication Skills
Principles of Effective Public Speaking
Principles of Effective Leadership
Advertising Women's Ministries
Women's Needs Assessments in the Local Church
Strategies for Evangelism

Electives (choose 3)
How to Study the Bible
Conflict Management
Self-Esteem
Organizing Retreats/Congresses
Professional Appearance and Deportment
Problem-Solving and Decision-Making Techniques
Goal-Setting/Visioning
Basic Writing Skills
Writing Letters
Teen Programs
Women's Ministries Needs Assessments in Local Community

Level 2

Core Requirements
Women of the Old Testament
Philosophy of Women's Ministries
Principles of Counseling
Presenting an Effective Seminar
Budget and Finance
Producing a Newsletter
Small Group Ministries and Support Groups
Reclaiming Former Members

Electives (choose 3)
Principles of Visitation
Audio-Visual Use/Production

Effective Leadership in Meetings, Committees, and Boards
Time Management
Program Building
Developing Your Resources
Writing Proposals
Prayer Ministries
Discipling New Members
Literacy Training
Assessing and Using Community Resources
Woman-to-Woman in Islam

Level 3

Core Requirements
Balancing Home and Career
Outreach Programs
Women's Role in Ellen White Writings
Women's Social and Legal Issues
Figures of Speech in the Bible
Women of the New Testament
Cultural Sensitivity

Electives (choose 3)
How to Prepare a Sermon
Fellowship Activities
Hospitality
Managing Volunteers
Mentoring
Personality Assessment
Public Prayer
Relating to Colleagues
Small-Group Dynamics
Spiritual Gifts
Writing with a Purpose

Level 4

Core Requirements

Leadership Mentoring for the 21st Century Woman

Women Mentoring Women

Christ's Mentoring Model

Creating Potential Leaders

Equipping Leaders for Success

The Nature of Relationship in Leadership

Women in Leadership in the Bible

Each level consists of core required seminars and a choice of electives; each seminar contains presenter's material and masters for handouts, overheads, and PowerPoint presentations. Upon completion, the participant will receive a certificate from her Union/Division Director. For more information, contact the Women's Ministries Department in your Conference/Union, or GC Women's Ministries at http://wm.gc.adventist.org.

Women's Ministries Programs in the Local Church

One of the most difficult aspects of Women's Ministries is program planning. How do we start? What kind of events should we feature? Whom should we target? Here are some ideas that may help you get started. Remember, you should always adapt ideas to your particular situation or members' needs. Meet with your committee and brainstorm for more ideas.

What is the purpose of these programs? To help women to grow spiritually. Therefore, when planning a program, it is important to see not only how the program will benefit women in the church, but how it can bring other women to the church. In these programs, all women can grow spiritually. But guests should also be encouraged to develop relationships that will bring them back to the church for evangelistic programs. This goal should always be kept in mind when planning programs.

Small Group Ministries for Women who:
- Want to know the Scriptures better (Bible studies)
- Want to be part of a prayer group
- Are seeking the fellowship of other women
- Are new converts
- Are single/single again

Support Groups for Women who are:
- Going through a divorce
- New mothers
- Mothers of teens
- Care-givers
- Single parents
- Grieving
- Victims of abuse
- Facing serious/terminal illness
- Overcoming addictions (smoking, alcohol, etc.)

Fellowship Opportunities:
- Exercise classes
- A night out (concert, eating out, plays, etc.)
- Neighborhood study groups
- Social opportunities that include spouses
- For women married to non-Adventists
- Moms in Touch
- The Widow's Mite

Women's Health Issues:
- Stop-smoking classes for women (Breathe-Free for Women)

- Weight-loss clinic
- Nutrition classes
- Cooking school
- Exercise groups
- Walking partners

Prayer Activities:
- Prayer Breakfasts
- Prayer Baskets
- Prayer Gardens (at home or church)
- Prayer Groups
- Prayer Partners
- Prayer Chains

Women's Ministries Outreach Activities in the Community

While all Women's Ministries activities should be carried out with an evangelistic intent, some programs may be planned specifically to attract community women. These programs could provide the foundation for upcoming evangelistic meetings.

- Neighborhood Christ-centered Bible study groups
- Inter-denominational Prayer Breakfasts
- International Women's Day of Prayer
- Vegetarian Cooking Classes
- Breathe-Free for Women
- Divorce Recovery
- Grief Recovery
- Scripture-Reading Day
- Meals for Kids
- Welcome Baby Program
- Literacy Programs
- Health Education for New Moms
- Financial Management

- Stress Reduction
- Prison Ministry
- Homes for AIDS Babies
- Crisis Hotline
- Homes for Battered Women

Support Groups Ministries

How to Start a Support Group

Suppose that some women from your local church Women's Ministries group came to you as the Women's Ministries Director and asked for help in starting a support group for them. They may be divorced women, overweight women, grieving women, women whose adult children have left the church—there are many possibilities. What do you do? Here are some suggestions:

Pray for guidance. You may wish to ask these women to pray with you.

Ask other interested persons to help you in framing up the plan. Conduct a survey to determine whether other women are interested in this particular topic.

Involve the pastor. Be sure he/she knows of your plans and ask for his/her advice or support. The pastor may suggest other interested persons or resources.

Choose a leader and others who are willing to help. A member of the group would probably make the best leader for the group.

If necessary, obtain permission from the Church Board. You will need this if you are requesting funds, church meeting rooms, etc. If you request funds, make a preliminary budget and submit it.

Set the time and place for your first meeting.

Study the needs of the group. What type of support do they need? Fellowship and support from each other? Experts to give advice? Inspiration and affirmation? You may want to do a survey of perceived needs. Plan a program to begin meeting these needs.

Plan the content of your program:
- Arrange for a speaker, facilitator, or activity.
- Include a devotional thought and prayer.
- Arrange for someone to open the room and have lights, room temperature, seating, etc.,
- Arrange for equipment such as projectors, public address systems, overhead projectors, paper, and pencils needed during the meeting.
- Provide refreshments if desired.
- If the meeting will involve parents with children, arrange for childcare.
- Remember to clean up after the meeting.

Advertise your first meeting. Use word-of-mouth, the telephone, the church bulletin, posters, and the Women's Ministries Newsletter—whatever works best for the group and the means available. But use *every* means you can—telling people something just once does not work any more.

Evaluate. After the meeting, meet with the leaders and discuss what went well. What needs to be planned before the next meeting? What needs to be changed? Make notes and discuss with your committee or assistants so you don't forget.

For an Effective Support Group	
DO	**DON'T**
• Provide opportunities for fellowship	• Allow gossiping or complaining
• Provide communication opportunities	• Promote or allow prejudice
• Maintain a biblical perspective	• Be cliquish
• Have an accepting attitude toward all	• Waste time
• Speak in a basic language so that all can understand	• Stray from the planned subject
• Maintain confidentiality	• Label people
	• Be judgmental

Mentoring

Heart-to-Heart promotes friendship between older and younger women. Titus 2:3-5 tells us that mature, godly women are responsible for teaching and discipling younger women.

A mature, godly woman's experience, empathy, maturity, and spirituality create an enormously powerful reservoir of untapped, God-given strength from which the church can benefit. Women need it; the Bible commands it. The Heart-to-Heart program taps this reservoir.

The following guidelines are suggested:

1. Make a one-year commitment to the relationship.
2. Contact each other once a week and meet at least once a month.
3. Pray for each other.
4. Do things together—study the Bible, shop, learn a new skill, or just go to lunch. Each set of partners is free to do what they want as long as they work on their relationship.

This is a ministry of encouragement, promoting friendships for support, counsel, and guidance. Because lives are changed through Christian love and support, families benefit, neighborhoods profit, and the entire church is blessed.

How to Start

The coordinator of Heart-to-Heart is a Women's Ministries Committee Board member; her primary function is to oversee the operation of the Heart-to-Heart ministry of senior and junior partners.

Administration

She shall select an assistant to help with administrative responsibilities:
- Matching senior/junior partners
- Making rematches when necessary
- Coordinating and publicizing social events

The coordinator and her assistant should use their knowledge of the women as well as the women's profile sheets to make matches. If possible, try to match women who are close geographically and have at least two interests in common.

There must be an appropriate age span between the partners. Generally, women under 35 are juniors; women 35-45 are either, and women 45 and older are seniors. Some women in their late twenties and thirties can be a senior to a younger woman but a junior to an older woman.

When a match is made, the senior initiates the first call to her junior, but from then on, calling should be shared equally between the two. The coordinator and/or her assistant should call the participating members in Heart-to-Heart monthly to find out how the matches are progressing. The coordinator should also keep a file of profile sheets, brochures, entertainment records, suggestions, etc.

Publicity

Have a one-month sign-up period.

- Make announcements and provide information and sign-up tables throughout the church.
- Place announcements in church bulletins and newsletters.
- Plan a Heart-to-Heart tea or luncheon to share experiences and to encourage others to join.

I Married a Possibility

There are many lonely women in our church today. Some feel cut off, disconnected, and lonely because they are married to non-believing spouses.

I MARRIED A POSSIBILITY (I.M.A.P.) provides an environment where small groups of women who share this commonality of being married to a "beloved unbeliever" can come together and find support.

The special focus of these small groups is to provide an atmosphere of acceptance and understanding and a sense of belonging, spiritual growth, and friendship. The formation of prayer partners is encouraged, and a prayer chain is utilized for specific needs. Members pray for each other's spouses and exchange phone numbers for conversations during the week.

By using the structure of relational Bible study and sharing common joys, struggles, and answers to prayer, new strength emerges to deal with daily difficulties.

Women no longer need to feel "spiritually single" and alone; this small-group ministry can provide them with friendships and support so that coming to church is a joyful, rather than a lonely experience. Members sit together and attend other church activities together, and this makes church more enjoyable for an I.M.A.P.

The group plans social activities in each other's homes, at parks, or in restaurants; spouses are sometimes invited. This social contact often begins to neutralize the spouse's resistance to the church and can lead to his joining the church family some day.

Divorce Recovery

The purpose of divorce recovery groups is to provide information, support, and friends who will listen without criticizing. With rising divorce rates, divorce victims need healing—in a non-judgmental, supportive environment. The church can provide this kind of help.

This suggested format is one that provides an opportunity to grow, share, and heal in an informative and supportive environment.

- Form a group of 10-11 people (maximum) who are seeking support through/after divorce.
- The first hour of the meeting is informative: a speaker, a panel, or interviews and testimonies.
- The second hour is spent with an experienced facilitator (leader). This is support, not therapy.
- Topics for discussions that have been the most helpful in these groups are:
    1. Accepting the reality of divorce and discussing the grief process—shock, denial, anger, and negotiating. Time alone does not heal. Support is needed through these steps, and friends can be the greatest help.
    2. Coping with loss and coping mechanisms available. Loss of self-esteem, security, a place in society, and one's new identity can be discussed.
    3. Unfinished business—denial, anger, fear, guilt, and being real and honest with these emotions.
    4. A new sense of family, helping the children cope.
    5. Forgiveness—the importance of being honest in the relationship. Sometimes group members are given the opportunity to write a letter (not neces-

sarily mailed) to the former spouse to help with the healing process.

6. Loneliness, dating, and intimacy in new relationships.

Widow's Ministry

The purpose of The Widow's Ministry is just that—to minister to hearts that are broken.

Goals

1. To reach out with love and understanding to those who have lost loved ones through death, particularly widows. To provide an atmosphere where they can express their grief and be ministered to.
2. To provide an understanding of the grieving process to those who are experiencing loss. To deal with this from a biblical perspective.
3. To provide a time when hurting people can meet together for fellowship, sharing of needs, Bible study, and prayer.
4. To help these experienced, gifted women to become active again by involving them in areas of the church where they feel comfortable.

Meeting frequency is determined by the local group, but most groups meet twice a month. Meetings are scheduled during the day or in the evening, depending on the age of the group members and the availability of transportation.

Life After Work:

Life After Work focuses on unreached working women. This ministry has become an important part of Women's Ministries.

Brown-Bag Bible Studies

Interdenominational Bible studies directed toward meeting the needs of working women who meet for lunch at work.

Light Lunches
Evangelistic messages presented by a guest speaker, shedding light on life in the working world. This is often a four- to eight-week mini-series.

Dinner Talks
Similar to Light Lunches.

Night Life
An evening of in-depth Bible study for working women who want to dig deeper into the Bible.

Life After Work
A large Monday-night meeting for working women; the meeting features songs, seminars, and a message relevant to the working world.

Sunday Breakfast Series
Special presentations on current topics delivered by experts in the field during a Sunday breakfast forum held at a local restaurant or fellowship room, approximately four times a year.

Moms' Circle of Love
Moms' Circle of Love is a group especially for mothers of preschoolers and young children.

What's a mother to do? To whom can she turn? Can the church assist those who feel overwhelmed, isolated, and stressed?

Young moms have so much to share with each other: a wealth of hands-on experience and broad shoulders for supporting each other. Because our hands stroke and pat the little heartbeats of the future, our eyes focus with a rich maternal vision. Let's use that vision to uplift, encourage, and promote the extraordinary challenge and art of mothering.

Information Questionnaire

Send out a questionnaire to the women in your church, informing them of your hope to form small Moms' Circle of Love groups (no more than 8-10 mothers per group). Ask them:

a) Would they be interested in attending?
b) How often would they attend?
c) What is the best time or day in the week?
d) Would they like to lead a MOMS group?
e) What role would they like a MOMS small group to fill for them as women?
f) What areas in their lives are the most neglected?

Possible Topics to Explore

Discipline	Burnout	Spiritual Gifts
Dysfunction	Grandparents	Mom's Night Out
PMS	Anger	Spiritual Growth
Crafts	Devotions	Time Management
Single Parenting	Postpartum	Stress Management
Fitness	Depression	
Daycare	Infertility	

Find good speakers who have expertise on these subjects.

Goals

We intend that the small Moms' Circle of Love groups will be places where mothers can develop special friendships and find others who understand their ups and downs.

Confidentiality is an important goal, and we also would hope that you would return to your roles refreshed and aware that you are not alone.

Source: Spruill, Karen. *Starting a Mothers' Support Group,* 1988.

Moms in Touch

What is *Moms in Touch*?

- It is two or more moms who meet for one hour each week to pray for their children, their children's schools, teachers, and school administrators.
- It is for mothers, grandmothers, or anyone who is willing to pray for a specific child in school.
- It is praying for students, preschool through college.
- It is for moms who believe that prayer makes a difference.

With the negative influence of television, music, and drugs in our schools today, we have found that a group of praying mothers is tremendously supportive and can make a great difference. These mothers have vision, direction, and faith. Their praying is very confidential. They spend their time praying, not talking, and they find promises to fit their needs. Some mothers take cookies to the school or meet with the faculty. This program has had a very positive influence on our schools.

The purpose of *Moms in Touch* is to intercede for our children through prayer and to pray that our schools may be guided by biblical values and high moral standards.

Lamentations 2:19 is the guiding text for Moms in Touch. It says, "Pour out your heart like water before the face of the Lord. Lift up your hands toward Him for the life of your children."

Small-Group Ministries

Purpose

Small-group ministries are an ideal way to meet women's needs. They can:

- Create networks of support for women with common needs and interests
- Build relationships
- Focus on spiritual growth

- Train for outreach
- Be accomplished without a budget—FREE!

Why are small groups an excellent tool for us?

The church is God's agent of reconciliation in the world, and it should be primarily concerned with bringing people together in healthy, growing relationships with God and others.

Small-Group Priority

Small groups should strive to help people and build them up. All efforts should aim to make us more loving, effective agents of reconciliation. If this takes place in the church, it will draw others to us.

Size of the Group

3-12 women = small group

15-40 women = medium-sized group

Six Types of Small Groups

1. **Sharing and Praying Group:** This group enjoys sharing experiences and answers to their prayers. They have a need to interact and verbalize.

2. **Bible Study Group:** This group emphasizes Bible study, marking their Bibles and completing assignments to be discussed with the group during the next session.

3. **Nurturing Group:** This small group is an excellent choice for newly-baptized members who want to make friends. It's even good for newcomers who are not members but want to enjoy Christian fellowship and growth in the Lord. This group enjoys Bible study, fellowship, and getting to know one another.

4. **Support Group:** This group of women shares a common bond. They may be divorced women, widows, per-

sons who have experienced abuse in their lives, singles, women married to non-believing spouses, etc. The small group focuses on similar needs.

5. **Outreach Group:** This group has a special interest in evangelism. They enjoy Bible study and all types of outreach endeavors. Let them be creative in what they do, but obtain the pastor's blessing before beginning any program that involves members or non-members.

6. **House Church Group:** This small group is comprised of people who cannot attend church for some reasons such as no church in their area, the nearest church is too far away, or for health reasons. People in these kinds of situations may be able to start a small group that would encourage others to stay involved.

Organizing a PALS Program (Prayer and Love Save)

Purpose of the PALS Program

The purpose of the PALS program is to encourage parents of adult children who have wandered from God and the church.

Scope of the PALS Program

The PALS program includes 11 lessons that are divided into three basic sections: accepting, loving, and praying,

Part I focuses on the reality of the situation and encourages parents to accept the things they cannot change, courage to change what they can, and the wisdom to know the difference when it comes to their relationships with their adult children.

Part II includes practical suggestions to help parents build better relationships with their adult children and their grandchildren.

Part III focuses on interceding for adult children who are prodigals. It offers prayer support for parents who have been hurt by the choices their adult children have made.

The final chapter makes suggestions for building a better future.

Program Schedule
The following is a suggested outline for using the material in a 70-minute group session.

Sharing Exercise ....10 minutes
Presentation of Topic ....15 minutes
Parent Showcase ....5 minutes
Handout on Topic
Small-Group Bible Study ....10 minutes
Group Discussion on Topic ....20 minutes
Prayer Time ....10 minutes

Organizational Structure
The material has been prepared so that the group leader can easily pick up the material and use it to lead a support/prayer group with a minimum amount of preparation

1. **Sharing Exercise**—This is a small-group "icebreaker" activity or whole-group interaction that is designed to put the members at ease or help them to think about the topic in an informal way.

2. **Presentation of the Topic**—This could be used as it is for a prepared talk, or it could be duplicated and distributed as an assigned reading before the next session. The content of the topic is vital for a meaningful discussion time and the related Bible-study activity.

3. **Parent Showcase**—This is a story of an actual parent or parents who put into practice the concept emphasized for the session.

4. **Handout on the Topic**—There is at least a one-page handout for each lesson.

5. **Bible Study**—These studies focus on a biblical parent(s) who faced a similar situation or applied the principle under discussion. If the group has more than eight members, divide into smaller groups of four to six for

this study. Everyone should have a copy of the Bible study page.

6. **Group Discussion**—The group leader can direct this discussion, or the group could be subdivided, with each member receiving a copy of the questions to be discussed.

7. **Prayer Time**—This is a time for parents to pray for each other and for their children or the children of others. It is a time of intercession that focuses on parents' concerns for their children and grandchildren.

Optional Uses of This Material

Weekly Prayer Group—This group could meet at the church or in someone's home at a convenient time.

Monthly Prayer Group—A monthly group may want to include more time for socialization, perhaps a supper or breakfast together before the lessons begin.

Sabbath School Alternative—This material could be used as a Sabbath School lesson study for one quarter.

Weekend Retreat—Plan a weekend retreat at a lodge, hotel, or conference camp facility. By doing two lessons on Friday evening, three on Sabbath morning, two on Sabbath afternoon, two on Sabbath evening, and two on Sunday morning, all of the lessons could be covered in a weekend.

Three Weekend Seminars—The seminars could include one or two sessions on Friday evening and another two or three on Sabbath afternoon, according to the segment of the program used.

Ministry Ideas

"God in Shoes"

"God in Shoes" is an innovative ministry started by the Women's Ministries Department of the Georgia-Cumberland Conference, North American Division, in 2004. With this ministry, a group of women go to an area in the conference that needs to have a concentrated ministry effort. They bring new shoes, gifts, and other resources needed to do ministry and make a difference in the community.

They also assist families with minor home repairs; deliver food supplies; host a Family Fun Day in the community; and give Bible studies.

"God in Shoes" Ministry is truly an innovative method of evangelism allowing "hands on" training for women to learn how to reach out into their communities. The women experience great joy doing ministry because it gives them an opportunity to touch lives and make a difference. They have each taken time to put together the food boxes and add personal items that give that extra touch and make it more than just a box of food.

Teen/Young Women's Ministry

In many parts of the world, Women's Ministry is reaching out to the young women in our churches ages 13 and up. The need to mentor our young women is evident no matter what country you are living in, but how do we bridge the gap between us? How can WM help our young women? What can you do to include them in your programs and ministry? Here are some ideas that we hope will help you answer these questions:

Begin by choosing as an assistant WM Leader who is a responsible young woman from your church.

As the chosen young woman, she has to establish her own Young WM Committee to meet and plan for the needs of the young women in the church.

The WM Leader of the church must be an advisor to this committee to guide them in their program planning, not to discourage them.

Sisters for Christ

Sisters for Christ (SFC) was established in January 2002 because a group of women were deeply concerned for the teenage girls of their church and surrounding community. They realized that these young girls were at risk because of the many challenges they faced such as sexual abuse, drug abuse, poor academic performance, mental health issues, depression, suicide, and teen pregnancies to name a few.

The concept is to create a safe place for the girls to meet and share their needs, concerns, and struggles, and to receive unconditional love and positive reinforcement.

A number of Adventist churches in America have adopted the Sisters for Christ program and the numbers are growing.

Project Ideas

Moms' Morning Out—Older women can minister to mothers by offering child-care programs for a few hours each week.

Prayer Breakfasts—This type of event provides time for women to share a meal, listen to an inspirational speaker, and share time in prayer.

Women's Evangelistic Meetings—Women are proving to be excellent evangelists though often with different perspectives and approaches. While some women hold traditional meetings featuring preaching, others are developing home Bible meetings.

Local Retreats—More Women's Ministries leaders are planning a day-long spiritual renewal retreat for women in their congregations (the women are encouraged to invite their non-Adventist friends). After the location is decided (hotel, park, church school, etc.), a keynote speaker is invited. Several workshops are planned, usually covering practical personal and spiritual topics like "How to Give Bible Studies," "Women's Health," or "Time Management." Special music is planned, and arrangements are made for meals. Time is included for fellowship and prayer.

Women's Day—Some churches enjoy devoting a Sabbath to honoring women. While the format varies, women usually lead out in Sabbath-morning services. After a meal (usually prepared by the men), the afternoon program may feature a concert or workshop or other special event such as a dramatic presentation about the contribution women have made to the church.

Reading Parties—Ask your guests to bring a short story, poem, or excerpt from their favorite book, writer, or story. Sit in a circle and ask each guest to read what she brought. Participants may choose to say something about what they are reading or just let the audience appreciate it as it is. Serve refreshments—cookies, hot soup, salad, drinks. This is the time to build friendships and to fellowship with other women as you learn about each other's interests.

Ministry to Nursing Homes—This outreach group could obtain the names of those from their church who are in nursing homes and then visit them, taking small remembrances such as flowers, cards, or cookies. Other ideas include having your women present special music or lead craft projects and Bible studies.

Adopt a Grandparent—This ministry might include visits in the home, taking an older person out occasionally for meals, or any other thoughtful gesture to brighten the life of an older person.

New Mothers—This ministry is for women in our church body or the community who have recently welcomed new babies into their homes, either by birth or adoption. Our purpose is to show support and encouragement with a personal visit to the hospital or the home.

Ministry Resources

- *Devotional Book Guidelines*
- *Leadership Certification Brochure*
- *Scholarship Program Brochure and PP presentation*
- *Women of Distinguished Service Brochure*
- *Mosaic Newsletter*
- *SOS Newsletter*
- *Organizing Support Groups in Your Church*
- *Leadership Certification Program*
  - *Level One*
  - *Level Two*
  - *Level Three*
  - *Level Four*
- *Advertising Women's Ministries* (Leadership Level One)
- *Producing a Newsletter* (Leadership Level Two)
- *Writing Proposals* (Leadership Level Two)
- *Public Prayer* (Leadership Level Three)
- *Writing with a Purpose* (Leadership Level Three)
- *Mentoring* (Leadership Level Three)
- *Personality Assessment* (Leadership Level Three)

(http://wm.gc.adventist.org or call (301) 680-6636)

CHAPTER SIX

Special Days for Women's Ministries

Special Days Calendar

- 1st Sabbath of March: International Day of Prayer

- 2nd Sabbath of June: Women's Ministries Emphasis Day

- 4th Sabbath of August: Abuse Prevention Emphasis Day

International Women's Day of Prayer

Since 1990, the General Conference Department of Women's Ministries has promoted a special day when women have the opportunity to strengthen their spiritual bonds as they pray for and with each other. The International Women's Day of Prayer is the first Sabbath of each March. In past years, this special day has been celebrated in a variety of ways: prayer breakfasts, fasting and prayer, consecration services, women preaching sermons for church services, and other special programs.

The International Woman's Day of Prayer provides an opportunity for women to learn about each other and pray for one another. It is a time to reunite with God and one another to strengthen spiritual bonds. Prayer for women everywhere creates a spiritual network of empathy and understanding between Adventist women. Thousands of women (and men) gather to pray on this day. Although the essential purpose of the day is prayer, the day can also provide women with an opportunity to strengthen their ties with other Christian women as they pray together.

Some may want to expand the day of prayer into a weekend prayer conference where participants can come to gain a deeper understanding of the need for prayer, its significance, blessings, and meaning in their lives. Weekend prayer conferences can address topics of interest such as: Bible prayers, how to pray scriptural promises, how fasting can enhance our prayer life, God's will and prayer, intercessory prayer, answered and unanswered prayer, closet prayers, and how to help our children develop a prayer life of their own.

Women's Ministries Emphasis Day

Women's Ministries Emphasis Day falls on the second Sabbath of each June. It is an opportunity for women to lead out in a worship service and a chance to educate the church regarding the purposes of Women's Ministries. It is an ideal time to introduce your leaders and committee to the church family and to invite women who have not been involved to join.

The Women's Ministries Leader should meet with the pastor at least six months prior to this day to discuss special plans for this Sabbath. This is an opportunity to plan a full day of activities, including Sabbath School, the Worship Service, a fellowship dinner, and perhaps an afternoon program. The leader may also want to use this time to honor women in the congregation who have done something unusual or outstanding. Resources for this purpose are available through the General Conference Women's Ministries Department.

Women's Ministries Emphasis Day
Available on the General Conference Web site; see www.wm.gc.adventist.og for an electronic version of the program.

Abuse Prevention Day

In 2001, the church voted to add an *Abuse Prevention Emphasis Day* to the church calendar of special Sabbaths, to occur on the fourth Sabbath in August. Women's Ministries works with Family Ministries, Health Ministries, Children's Ministries, the Youth Department, and the Ministerial Association to prepare materials for the prevention emphasis day.

This emphasis day provides an opportunity for local churches to address the issue of abuse, educates church members and leadership, and lets victims know that their church cares.

Women's Ministries directors in the local churches should plan very early so that this day can be included on the local church calendar. Work closely with your pastor to keep him/her informed.

Ministry Resources
- *International Day of Prayer* – First Sabbath of March (Packet online)
- *Women's Ministries Emphasis Day* – Second Sabbath of June (Packet online)
- *Abuse Prevention Day* – Fourth Sabbath of August (Packet online)
- *Abuse Posters*
- *Breaking the Silence Brochures* (Six)
    - You can stop the violence and help them heal
    - Do you know someone who is abused?
    - Are you being abused by your boyfriend or husband?
    - Are you abusing someone?

    - Has your child been abused?

    - Are you being abused by your girlfriend or wife?

- NEW Abuse Brochure: *Love Shouldn't Hurt: Resources for Pastors*
- *HIV/AIDS Teaching Material* – CD ROM, PDF, Flip Chart, Presentation for overheads, Power Point Presentation.
- *Illiteracy: How to Begin a Literacy Program* – Ardis Stenbakken (Seminar)

(http://wm.gc.adventist.org or call (301) 680-6636)

CHAPTER SEVEN

Evangelism

Evangelism takes many shapes and forms. In this section you will find a focus on One-to-One Bible Study, Small Group Evangelism, Seminar Style Evangelism and finally the importance of Discipling New Members.

Evangelism Ministry Ideas

A. One-to-One Bible Study

One of the most satisfying spiritual ministries is that of giving personal Bible studies. It takes time and energy, but you will find it one of the most rewarding and challenging experiences of life.

How does a person find someone with whom to study the Bible? These people may be receptive relatives, neighbors, contacts in the community, the workplace, or a friend who has been watching your life and seeing that you have a peace and joy they would like to have.

The two-by-two plan, as the Lord sent out disciples, is the best way to give Bible studies. That way one can encourage the other, and you can counsel, pray, and search the Bible together.

For Effective Bible Study

Giving Bible studies is not as hard as most imagine, and one does not have to be a Bible scholar to be successful. The number one secret of effective Bible study is prayer

What You Need

Before you can teach others, it is also helpful to have some materials yourself. Helpful source materials for One-to-One Bible studies include a Bible, a Bible Concordance, and Bible Guides. Study guides help to keep the Bible study focused and moving, therefore keeping the interest of the Bible student and keeping on the subject.

- It is helpful if you can meet regularly so that your student can look forward to your visit.
- Try to make the study time as clear as possible. And it is also helpful if you can schedule the study for the same time, once each week.
- Don't make the study long—no more than one hour—minimize the amount of information that is given, giving time for application. Most people can't concentrate for longer than that.
- Don't give the student an excuse to decide that he or she doesn't have the time to study because it takes too much time.
- It is also important for you to arrive at the scheduled hour so that you can take a few minutes to get better acquainted with your student at each study hour, and that you take time for prayer before introducing the subject of study.
- After the study of the lesson, it is important to invite a commitment and have a commitment prayer.
- Encourage a commitment at each Bible study.
- Share your personal testimony, briefly, by telling your experience before you met Christ, how you met Christ, and the joy you have found since you met Christ. Keep your personal testimony brief—from two to four minutes.

- Help the student to understand that all of us need the grace of Christ, so realize that those who worship with you are not perfect.

Organization of a Bible Study

There are five principle parts to a Bible study:

- *Get acquainted time...* Your Bible student must become your friend. So take a few minutes at the beginning of each study time to deepen your friendship.

- *Introduce the lesson and pray...* A short introduction of your subject of study will help your student to know the purpose of the study. Then begin your study time with a sincere prayer, asking for the Holy Spirit's guidance in your study of God's Word.

- *Lesson study...* The question and answer approach, as well as allowing the student to read the Bible text answer, will help to keep the interest of the student. It will also help to establish confidence in the Word of God. Avoid disagreeing on a point of doctrine until you have had time to study it thoroughly from the Bible. It may be explained in a future lesson. It is important to remember that it is the work of the Holy Spirit to convince the student of his or her need of Christ and His teachings. Whatever subject is being presented, uplift Jesus as the center of all hope. Remember, the wonderful love of Christ will reach the heart when the mere reiteration of doctrine would accomplish nothing.

- *Commitment and prayer...* Begin with the very first lesson to ask a commitment question at the conclusion of your study time. You may often give a brief personal testimony that will encourage your student in his or her commitment. Seal the commitment with prayer. Encourage your student to pray when he/she feels comfortable doing so.

- *Next appointment time and leaving...* It is best to leave immediately after your prayer time, except to confirm your next appointment time. At the appropriate time, you will want to invite your student to attend church or an evangelistic meeting with you.

B. Small Group Evangelism

One of the most successful types of Bible studies is the Small Group study. There are a number of reasons for its success:

- People are often less intimidated by small groups and more willing to share
- It can be held in more convenient, close-to-home locations
- The group can provide a feeling of caring and nurture
- People have a better opportunity to study at their own pace
- The Small Group creates a natural group for continued discipling

When planning for a Small Group study, it is essential to include five areas:

1. Sharing–getting acquainted
2. Bible study–learning about God's Word
3. Prayer–asking for God's assistance
4. Social time–meeting outside the group
5. Service–doing something for someone else

Before inviting people to a group for Bible Study, begin with prayer that God will attract the group members He wants, and that He will enable you to lead and encourage the group.

One of the goals of a Small Group Bible study is to create an atmosphere of love and acceptance which stimulates discoveries and freedom to speak about the Bible without fear of embarrassment or criticism. This will foster positive Christian fellowship.

C. Seminar Style Evangelism

Seminar style evangelism is more formal than One-on-One

Bible studies or relational small groups but not as formal as a full scale evangelistic meeting. Seminar style invites more dialogue and participation than you would ordinarily have in an evangelistic meeting.

There are four vital keys to the success of any evangelistic endeavor, but especially important when conducting seminars:

- Prayer partners praying for the success of each and every meeting, even while the meeting is going on.
- People need to hear you say over and over again that you interpret the Bible (for example Daniel) by what the Bible says; that you let the Bible explain itself. We don't go by human teachings, we don't listen to preachers, we don't look at current events to find how to interpret the Scriptures . . . we let the Bible explains the Bible.
- It is of utmost necessity that you make clear to people who are coming to the seminar *that your purpose is to uplift Jesus Christ.* Talk about Jesus; let the folk know that you love Jesus, that you have a personal relationship with Him, and that you want them to have that same personal relationship with Jesus. This cannot be overemphasized. An intimate relationship with Jesus is vital for them to go through the end time and enter into the Kingdom of Heaven.
- Share with them that our purpose in studying last-day events is not to just have a detailed understanding of the last days, but also to help them be prepared for that time.

The Evangelistic Team at Work

It is not wise to try to do an evangelistic seminar by yourself. Others need the experience as well as the blessing.

If you are asked to help with registration, or with setting up or tearing down of the seminar, remember that those jobs are secondary. Your first priority is to build relationships with the people who come.

D. Discipling New Members

Women are intimately involved in the birth process. Almost all women love babies and most of the care for babies is done by women. So it seems entirely appropriate that women should be involved in the process of discipling. But any woman who has had a baby will also tell you that giving birth is painful and raising children is hard work.

In Matthew 28, Jesus tells us to do four things: 1) go; 2) make disciples; 3) baptize; and 4) "teach them to obey everything I have commanded you." As a church, we do well with numbers one and three; we do fairly well with number four before baptism, but after baptism, we do not teach or disciple very well. This is one of the reasons we lose so many members.

Helping New Members Feel at Home

People resist change because change is hard. But when people are baptized, we ask them to change churches, or if they have not been a church member, to become one, an even harder change. We ask them to change their day of worship, the food they eat, what they drink, their recreation, sometimes their friends, and perhaps their jobs. We need to be patient and helpful during this process.

One of the best ways to help them face all this change is to help them become mature Christians, and to be their friend or at least see to it that they have new friends.

Ideas

- Have a new member committee – This committee is responsible for the integration of new members. They would also assign special friends (spiritual guardians) to each new member, and monitor them to see that they are functioning.
- New member banquet – Meet once or twice a year where new members are featured. The special friends would in-

troduce these new members to the congregation and tell them about their interests, hobbies, and how they came into the church, etc. This committee should have members that are new members.

- New member visitation –
    1. Once a week during the first month
    2. Once a month for the first year
    3. Leave special books: morning watch books, Spirit of Prophecy books, magazines, *I Chose Adventism, Beyond Baptism*, etc.
- Watch for any indication of problems or adjustment (such as: absence from Sabbath School or church service, or a failure to make friends). Don't be surprised at what some may do even after baptism. It is difficult to change lifestyles overnight. Be kind. Don't condemn. Stay with them. Keep them reading and studying.

Training and Equipping New Members

A person is not really a full participating member until he/she becomes a reproducing disciple. If we want disciples in our church, we will need to teach them before the baptism and teach as well as train them afterwards. This training should include:

- Further classes in doctrines. People cannot comprehend the whole message the first time that they hear the gospel.
- Special classes for the new believers could be held during Sabbath School class time, or prayer meeting time, or Sabbath afternoons—any time that is convenient for the new believers.
- Teach them how to study the Bible and pray. There are many good books and seminars on prayer and Bible Study.

But most of all it is important to actually study the Bible and pray with them, first modeling how it is done and then helping them pick out the Bible topics and books or chapters they would like to study, and coaching them through it.

Project B=B: Bible Equals Baptism

Several years ago, Edit Fonseca from the Southern Parana Conference in Brazil dreamed of and began a Bible study program she called Project B=B or Bible=Baptism. It has been highly successful, and many have been baptized throughout South America as a result. It is an excellent way to give the women opportunities to work for their family, friends, and neighbors in One-on-One Bible studies.

The Project

First, there is prayer. Women pray specifically about Project B=B in their Women's Ministries meetings. They pray before the project begins, during the initial stages of the project, and as the project continues.

Next, they schedule an interview with the pastors/elders to explain the project and to negotiate the purchase of Bibles through the church or other means. Schedule the date of this event. The date should be on any Sabbath during the first part of the year, so that there will be enough time to finish all of the Bible studies by the end of the year. Preference could be given to one of the two special dates for Women's Ministries that are already on the church calendar:

- 1st Sabbath in March: International Women's Day of Prayer
- 2nd Sabbath in June: Women's Ministries Emphasis Day

They then prepare their material, copying the Project B=B enrollment card to be handed to each person who participates (See page 94 for sample.)

After a date is finalized, they begin to advertise the date.

The program can include testimonies, congregational singing, special songs, informative talks about Women's Ministries, local and worldwide Women's Ministries news, interviews, and depositions.

The Women's Ministries Director or another person speaks about the joy of sharing Christ's message with others.

She immediately asks each person present (women, men, youth, elderly) to think of a relative or friend who would be happier if they study the Word of God. She then explains that Women's Ministries has a plan to help reach these people. She emphasizes that each person who participates takes a Bible, Bible Study guides, and a baptismal certificate. The Leadership and Planning Committee then asks each person to make a commitment to:

- Study the Bible with one person
- Prepare this person for baptism by the end of the year.

The Bible and the Bible studies do not belong to the person who received them in the church, but to the person who needs to be reached by the message.

The name of the person who will receive the Bible studies will become part of the prayer list at the Wednesday evening worship and/or the women's prayer group prayer list.

Each person who takes a Bible and Bible studies will be supervised in their missionary work by the Women's Ministries Leader of the church, mission, or conference. These directors will regularly send correspondence and bulletins, or they will maintain contact by phone. Whenever a doubt or difficulty arises during the studies, immediate help can be received because of this regular contact.

The Bible student is asked to study in the new Bible without underlining, marking, or writing even his or her name. The Bible will not permanently belong to the interested person until the day of her or his baptism or graduation. (Some people may decide to be baptized long after the studies have concluded.)

When someone who is studying the Bible asks to be baptized, this person should be directed to the pastor. The baptismal form should be filled out, and this person should be informed about the baptismal ceremony. Any doctrinal questions that this person may have should be clarified

Closing Ceremony

Not only do women have a special service to begin Project B=B, but they also participate in a special ceremony for the closing/baptismal service. They organize the Bibles and Bible studies on a front table. They have the Project B=B enrollment cards and the baptismal certificates on hand.

The Bible should be wrapped in beautiful paper with a lovely bow, and given after the baptism to the person who studied it. A Bible Marking Plan should be given with the Bible. You may want to write a dedication in the Bible.

Those in charge of the program request that those who took the Bible and the Bible studies remain in the front after they have heard the above instructions and have filled out and returned the Project B=B Enrollment card. All are asked to raise their Bible and the Bible studies high. A Bible promise is read, and if possible, a picture is taken of the group. Then the pastor is invited to say a few words to motivate the group and to offer a prayer of consecration for the group and their work.

The Discipleship Begins

Then discipleship begins. After the baptism, a class of new members can be formed, or these new members can study individually. However, this time the study will follow the Bible Marking Plan. Students will be taught how to use this plan correctly. This reinforces the topics learned before baptism. It prepares new members to teach others.

After completing the Bible Marking Plan, a graduation may be held. Certificates for the completed course will be given along with a new Bible and a series of the Bible studies, a Project B=B Enrollment card, and a blank Baptismal Certificate, so that the new member can continue with Project B=B.

Enrollment Card for
Project B=B (Bible = Baptism)

Personal information for the individual who will receive studies

Name _____

Age _____ Marital Status _____

Current Religious Affiliation _____

Is this person a member of a Sabbath School class?_____

Is this person a member of the Bible Study class? _____

Instructor responsible _____

Name _____

Name of the Seventh-day Adventist Church you attend _____

_____

Name of Your Pastor _____

Is it possible for women to be involved in evangelism?

Absolutely! Yes! Will the world be warned without women taking an active part? Not in our lifetime, or perhaps ever! Let us let the Holy Spirit, that wonderful gift from the Lord, burn in our hearts, empowering us to help finish the work, to hasten the coming of the Lord.

Ministry Resources

- *Evangelism Manual* (www.AdventSource.com)
- *Prayer and Loves Saves* (For Parents)
- *Discipling New Members* – Jean Sequeira (Seminar)
- *Bible Study for Busy Women*

- *How to Study the Bible* (Leadership level One)
- *Principles of Visitation* (Leadership Level Two)
- *Prayer Ministries* (Leadership Level Two)
- *Woman to Woman in Islam* (Leadership Level Two)
- *How to Prepare a Talk/Sermon* (Leadership Level Three)
- *Outreach Programs* (Leadership Level Three)
- *Small Groups Dynamics* (Leadership Level Three)
- *My Spiritual Gifts* – Rose Otis (Seminar)
- *Spiritual Growth For Today's Women* - Rose Otis (Seminar)
- *Women Discovering Jesus* – Lea Hardy (Seminar)
- *Desire, Discover, Depend On, and Do the Word* – Dorothy Watts (Seminar Guide and Workbook)

(http://wm.gc.adventist.org or call (301) 680-6636)

Web Sites

World Church
www.adventist.org

Seventh-day Adventist Beliefs
www.adventist.org/beliefs

General Conference Women's Ministries
http://wm.gc.adventist.org

Resources
www.adventsource.org

Adventist Organizations Online
www.adventistsingleadultministries.org
www.advenstistfamilyministries.org
www.saltyfish.net
www.plusline.org

www.aidsministry.com
www.hesaidgo.net
www.yp4him.org
www.reviewandherald.com

Articles and Web Sites
Spiritual Gifts Summary
www.nisbett.com/sgifts

Ministry Areas Using Your Spiritual Gifts
http://mintools.com/ministries

Singles and Evangelism
www.gbod/evangelism/programs